Anna MANCINI

COPYRIGHT LAW

IS OBSOLETE

Buenos Books America

ISBN-10: 1-932848-20-7 (HARDCOVER)
ISBN-13 : 978-1-932848-20-5 (HARCOVER)
ISBN-10: 1-932848-18-5(PAPERBACK)
ISBN-13: 9781932848182 (PAPERBACK)
ISBN-10:1-932848-19-3 (E-BOOK)
ISBN-13: 978-1-932848-19-9 (E-BOOK)
Also in French and Spanish
Published by:
BUENOS BOOKS AMERICA, Dover, DE
info@BuenosBooks.us
http://www.buenosbooks.us

E-books available on our Websites:

WWW.BUENOSBOOKS.US

Library of Congress Control Number: 2006922777

Also in French and Spanish

CONTENTS

PART 2   61
LEGAL PROPOSALS
TO HELP DEVELOP
THE VIRTUAL BOOK MARKET

4

INTRODUCTION

The Internet, e-books, print-on-demand and Digital Rights Management technologies are profoundly changing the economics of the book market. For the first time in the history of the humankind, we have acquired a new technology capable of making books available to everyone as digital files or even as physical books. Indeed, when they are sufficiently distributed throughout the world, print-on-demand technologies will allow us to create physical books from digital files wherever we wish. We will no longer have to suffer the heaviness and limitations linked to the material world. It will be much easier to circulate books as digital files and to print them where we want on reader demands, than to transport and stock printed books. The emerging virtual book market is very different from the traditional book market. The laws of the virtual economy are vastly different from the laws of the material economy, to which we are accustomed and which have shaped our legal systems.

In the first part of this book, we will observe the changes occurring in the book market. We will discuss the choices of society, even of civilization, provided by the use, appropriate or otherwise, of new communication technologies. We will reflect on possible restrictions to the free-flow of ideas that could result from use contrary to the purpose of communication technologies.

In the second part of this book, we will explain why some legal concepts such as intellectual property or the traditional idea of justice are unsuited to the new emerging book market. We will then propose other solutions. Finally, we will propose guidelines to modernize copyright law so that it can help the emerging book market to move toward the creation of a civilization of freedom of speech and information abundance for all, as well as the highest respect for authors.

PART 1

THE RAPID CHANGES IN THE BOOK MARKET

OPPOSED TO THE RIGIDITY OF LAW

CHAPTER 1

A philosophy of law severed from reality

The globalization involved in the technological progress is profoundly changing the publishing world. Copyright, however, has not been adapted to this. Changes that have been regularly proposed in domestic or international copyright laws are not in proportion to the importance of the changes taking place in the book market. This is mainly due to the fact that Governments and lawyers are overwhelmed by immediate problems and are attempting to find solutions for each new case, under great pressure from lobbying groups and without time for philosophical distance. Worldwide, legal changes are limited to patching up the existing copyright law. However, the profound change currently taking place in the publishing industry requires a deeper philosophical thinking to enable the efficient update of copyright law and to help make the right collective choices. Indeed, in the short term, thanks

9

to technology, humanity could for the first time in history have the choice between an almost free worldwide flow of books or its opposite: the total control of this flow by countries or private entities in possession of the most sophisticated technology. In order that new technologies are used to foster the free flow of ideas and the progress of knowledge, States worldwide should enter into international agreements inspired by long-term cultural objectives. In the long term, what is now at stake with copyright law is little compared to what awaits us. This is why we need deep philosophical thinking on this issue that is not limited to the timely problems of the book market. Moreover certainly the best way to more effectively resolve these present problems is to examine the entire problem from a distance. In the past, philosophers have efficiently inspired governments in the field of copyright law. KANT, for example, had a strong influence on German copyright law. As for French law, it was directly inspired by philosophers and writers of the French Revolution era. This law was so well conceived that it remained in effect for more than 160 years without significant amendments. Nowadays, due to its complexity, the philosophy of law has become the preserve of specialized lawyers. Due to this fact, philosophers generally no longer discuss specialized legal issues. As for philosophers of law, it is no longer possible to rely on them to adapt the law to the fast pace of changes occurring in the modern world. Indeed, since the 19th century, they have been confined to the limits imposed by legal positivism. In France, for example, legal positivism has become the dominant legal "religion" and the heretical are simply excluded from universities, research, academic publishing and academic journals. According to this philosophy, lawyers are supposed to limit themselves to knowledge of the law and to the determination of the applicable law to a specific legal problem. The lawyer's job is only that. In other words, according to this philosophy, a lawyer is not authorized to observe the real world, to think about what is justice, and even less to be creative. Lawyers should know only the positive law and apply it the best they can. Due to such a philosophy, it is not surprising that, most of the time, legal thinkers content themselves with the exegesis of the existing law and case law, without closely observing the new realities of the book market. In doing so, they are unable to propose the innovations made necessary by the extent of the changes

11

taking place in the publishing world. In Europe, lawyers tend to remain entrenched in the existing law without sound knowledge of the book market. In America, some legal thinkers have a better knowledge of the market but remain trapped in the existing law for lack of philosophical distance. In France, official reports on copyright law have raised "positivist" questions focused on the positive laws and on their suitability to new situations. This is to such an extent that one would wonder if prophets also revealed the laws of the State!

For example, in a report entitled "Le droit d'auteur et l'Internet" (Copyright law and the Internet), it states:

> "The aim of this report is to analyze the consequences on copyright law brought about by this new means of communication (=Internet) and to see what the situation is regarding copyright and neighboring rights in the field of the new communication technologies." [1]

It is interesting to quote this report in order to illustrate the way modern positivistic lawyers tend to think about new problems.

"Actually, it seems that in the digital environment, the strong principles of copyright and neighboring rights call for a slight adaptation rather than to be turned upside down."[2]

And the report comes to the conclusion that:

"For sure, present copyright law applies to the Internet...."[3]

Until now, in the field of philosophy of law there have been no in-depth studies based on the observation of the functioning of the emerging virtual and global book market. Due to the lack of such studies, European Governmental reports remain strongly influenced by the positivist approach to law and generally lead to this kind of conclusion:

"Finally, the application of copyright law is not impossible. But in practice, it encounters many difficulties. The traditional components of copyright laws are turned upside down... even the determination of the applicable law is not easy. However, laws exist for all the questions previously raised."[4]

Having studied the specialized literature, we have come to the conclusion that there are no legal voids for treating questions raised by new technologies in the field of

13

copyright. Instead, the void is philosophical and mainly due to the obsolescence of the traditional legal positivism.

In a time of rapid technological changes, legal positivism means a deficiency of philosophy of law. Without philosophical thinking, lawyers can no longer help create the law, and inspire the governments to more effectively solve unprecedented practical problems. Legal positivism does indeed imply that lawyers always look at past laws to solve new legal problems. Nevertheless, technological progress in communication devices has created an unprecedented gap between the economic world that was the background of the legal positivism and the new virtual economy created by the Internet. The economic world in which the legal positivism was born was marked by materialism and stability. Such an economic context allowed for the practical efficacy of legal positivism, just as it limited the needs for legal innovation. The laws of the virtual economy are totally opposed to the laws of the economic world that gave birth to legal positivism. From this fact, such a philosophy is useless in this new context and we are going to adopt a different approach to the problem of copyright in the emerging virtual book market.

First, instead of looking at the existing law to check if it can be applied to the new problems, we will examine the realities of the present book market. For this purpose, we will study the history of the book from Antiquity until the present day in order to define what is actually a book. Then, we will observe the ongoing transformations of the book market, its increasing virtualization and globalization. In order to better understand these transformations, we will take the examples of two fictitious States in two different countries, which have adopted opposing approaches to the virtualization of the book market. Through these two examples, we will study the consequences of these two ways of using new communication technologies and the Internet.

CHAPTER 2

The evolution of the concept of book from Antiquity until the present day

1: The book as voice substitute

Studies regarding the history of the book generally speak about the physical changes of books over time, from papyrus to the modern e-book. In so doing, they forget the first "shape" of books, which was verbal. Literature on the history of books forgets to mention the long-lasting tradition of the verbal transmission of knowledge and the fact that the spoken word preceded the book. Indeed, the first books were considered to be a substitute of the spoken word. In other words, in these studies little or no room is left for the "intangible book", that is to say to the totally intangible book which circulates directly among people without objects other than their own bodies. Speech as such, and thought, are the roots of all existing books that have only served as a means of materializing

17

them. The thoughts exchanged by human beings thanks to the spoken word came before tangible books. All existing shapes of books have been simply a means for materializing these thoughts initially transmitted through the sound. Before the advent of writing, the beginnings of the humankind were marked by a tradition of verbal transmission of knowledge. Many primitive people considered human speech a living thing that, through its circulation among people, made life energy circulate too. This approach to the spoken word can be seen in Plato's works, in which Socrates assimilates a discourse to a seed that is more efficient that the written discourse, and Phaedrus asserts:[5]

"Phaedrus: You mean the living word of knowledge which has a soul, and of which written word is properly no more than an image? "

"Soc. True, Phaedrus. But nobler far is the serious pursuit of the dialectician, who, finding a congenial soul, by the help of science sows and plants therein words which are able to help themselves and him who planted them, and are not unfruitful, but have in them a seed which others brought up in different soils render immortal, making the possessors of it happy to the utmost extent of human happiness."

18

As for the ancient Egyptians, studies of Maat the Goddess of Justice show that they considered the spoken word to be solar energy received through the heart, transformed by the human being and emitted through the tongue. (In other words, through speech).[6] In ancient legal systems, the spoken word was supposed to create legal links between people and legal obligations. We know, for example, that in the Ancient Roman Law, ritual legal formulae had to be accurately articulated before the pontiffs who rendered justice. If not, the legal process was void.[7]

Contrary to primitive people, modern man gives more importance to written texts than to the spoken word. Before a tribunal, a written proof has more value than a verbal promise. All our legal tradition is marked by the supremacy of the written laws. In the same way, all our cultural tradition is marked by the preeminence of writing and by the increasing importance assumed by the book as an object separate from its author.

The civilization of writing has permitted the author to be separated from his thoughts through the materialization of thought. This was not possible in the verbal tradition.

19

Being materialized, the thought became an object that can be owned. However, the transition from the tradition of verbal transmission of knowledge to its written transmission has not been easy. Socrates, for example, was reluctant and granted a higher value to verbal communication than to the written book. He believed that writing was not as suitable as the spoken word to transmit the author's message. In Plato's Phaedrus, it states: [8]

> "Socrates: I cannot help feeling, Phaedrus, that writing is unfortunately like painting; for the creations of the painter have the attitude of life, and yet if you ask them a question they preserve a solemn silence. And the same may be said of speeches. You would imagine that they had intelligence, but if you want to know anything and put a question to one of them, the speaker always gives one unvarying answer. And when they have been once written down they are tumbled about anywhere among those who may or may not understand them, and know not to whom they should reply, to whom not: and, if they are maltreated or abused, they have no parent to protect them; and they cannot protect or defend themselves."

The transition between the "spoken book" and the written book occurred slowly. For a long time, written books continued to be considered as a simple imperfect substitute for the human voice. People continued to read it aloud because the sound seemed more important to them than the written words. The silent reading of books took place little by little and involved the decline of the tradition of the verbal transmission of knowledge. At this point in history, readers could directly access knowledge without the mediation of authors. Despite all the progress made, the imperfection of the book in comparison to human speech was often alleged. To the first readers, books were above all messages and not tangible objects.

2: The book as a message, as a means of communicating ideas

SAINT AUGUSTINE[9] underlined the fact that books allowed communication with those absent, and the Greek historian DIODORUS believed that writing permitted communication between the living and the dead, and between people situated in remote locations.[10] When in the 18th century, Immanuel KANT wrote:

> "A book is a writing which contains a discourse addressed by someone to the public, through visible signs of speech. It is a matter of indifference to the present considerations whether it is written by a pen or imprinted by types, and on few or many pages. He who speaks to the public in his own name is the

author. He who addresses the writing to the public in the name of the author is the publisher."[11]

He had certainly noticed the difference between a book as an object and the message it contained. As early as the 18th century, however, the tangible aspect of the book already prevailed over its intangible attributes. This was mainly due to economic reasons, as we will see below.

3: The tangible book as an object of a property

In the course of history, the high price of printed books and their scarcity caused the tangible aspect of books to prevail over their intangible side. Above all, the book was then considered as an object to be owned, an object on which a right of property was borne. We know that in the 12th century, a copy of the Bible could equal the price of a city house[12] and that in 1374, King Edward III of England paid the price of three London houses for one book.[13] From 1450 the invention of printing by GUTENBERG allowed a notable decrease in the price of books and the multiplication of copies. This significantly increased the number of readers who could afford to own books.

Nowadays, despite the even greater decrease in the price of books and the abundance of printed books on the market, books are still perceived as objects. This is particularly obvious in the field of law. Copyright laws worldwide are focused on the tangible aspect of books, while in the emerging virtual book market their intangible aspect is returning to the stage. The fact that, in the virtual book market, books have recovered their intangible nature renders obsolete many aspects of copyright laws.

In other words, in the virtual book market, the book as a digital file transmitted through the Internet is no longer the tangible object we are used to handling physically, philosophically and legally.

On legal grounds, this means that a digital book can no longer be classified in the same legal categories as tangible books. We will study this in greater detail in the second part of this book. For now, we are going to determine what are the fundamental differences between the traditional book market and the virtual book market.

CHAPTER 3

The fundamental differences between the traditional book market and the virtual book market

In a previous study about Internet law, we analyzed in detail the differences between the traditional world (without the Internet) and the virtual world of the Internet.[14] The same observations apply to the difference between the printed book market and the virtual book market (that is to say, the market of digital books transmitted worldwide through the Internet). At this point we will not enter into a detailed analysis. These differences will appear better through the example of two fictitious States opposed in their approach to the virtual book market. One of these States would use the potentiality of virtual publishing in order to speed up the flow of information; while the other would desperately try to continue the old way, despite the possibilities offered by new communication technologies. Through these two examples, we will explain the functioning of the print-on-demand technologies, and we will see how, in conjunction with the Internet, they are radically changing the business model of the book market.

1: The constraints of the tangible side of the book market and their legal, economic and cultural consequences

In the traditional book market, the physicality of books involves legal and practical consequences that are no longer true in the virtual book publishing. From a legal standpoint, for example, the concept of property naturally applies to tangible things, among them the book as an object, even if books are only the materialization of intangible thoughts. As a tangible object, a book can be spatially localized. We know where it was made and can follow its path from publisher to reader. The concept of territory being the cornerstone of all modern legal systems, the sole fact that we can localize a book-object involves many legal and tax consequences.

The territorial partition of the printed book market allows States to exert control over the flow of ideas on their territories. In other words, as soon as ideas are

26

materialized in physical books, the flow of ideas can be easily controlled. Hence, in the traditional book market, there are many limitations to the free flow of ideas within the same territory due to political, economic or cultural reasons. In the same way, economic laws which bear on material goods (customs rights, shipping fees, inventories) slow down the domestic and international flow of ideas. Due to all these constraints linked to the tangible aspect of books, many authors are excluded from the book market. Indeed, this market cannot publish every single author for reasons that, today, are mainly economic. Either the publication is not profitable because it does not meet a broad enough audience, or it cannot enter any of the usual distribution channels. Due to the financial risks involved by the physicality of books, publishing companies can publish only authors whose work is financially interesting. While censorship in the publishing industry was previously largely political, today it has become largely economic. This "economic censorship" eliminates all books from the market which are not profitable. The stakes of old times have been replaced by the laws of the market, combined with some disguised measures of censorship that still exist, even in the most liberal

27

countries. Most of the time, nowadays, non-commercial books are published outside of the market, by universities, non-profit organizations, and research centers, all generally subsidized by governments. Due to financial constraints in traditional publishing, the choice of titles on offer today in the commercial sector is becoming narrower and narrower. In virtual publishing, this logic is reversed.

2: Virtual publishing: a market free from the territoriality criterion and its legal consequences

Unlike printed books, whose physicality slows down their circulation, digital books are free from all obstacles linked to matter: extremely low production and distribution costs compared to printed books, no inventory costs, no limitations due to space. Thanks to the Internet, digital books can travel worldwide, free from territorial links. This fact, added to the intangibility of digital books, makes many territory-based legal concepts inapplicable to the virtual market. Indeed, these traditional legal concepts are suited to books as objects circulating in territory-based book markets, but not to intangible books circulating worldwide.

The virtual publishing market shows the uselessness of the territory criterion, and yet this criterion is the cornerstone of all modern legal systems and philosophies. The most common legal concepts, such as property (invented for tangible objects), theft (implying the physicality of the stolen object and the usefulness of returning it to its legitimate owner), and seizure of counterfeit goods (which presupposes the existence of tangible items that can be seized) are no longer applicable in the context of the virtual publishing market. Also, censorship can no longer rely on the facilities provided by the physical aspect of books. Economic censorship, which nowadays is the most drastic kind, no longer has reason to exist in the virtual book market, where it costs very little to publish a new author and distribute her or his works worldwide. Digital publishing broadens the choice available to the public. People themselves choose, instead of being limited by the drastic choice imposed by traditional publishing companies. The number of titles available in the virtual book market is multiplied and their purchase price can be considerably reduced. This constitutes *per se* an acceleration of the circulation of the flow of ideas. While the traditional publishing market tends to be territory-based, virtual publishing is free from territories and borders. Thanks to its intangibility, the digital book travels throughout the world in a few seconds, and the automated secure payment system allows it to be sold everywhere where people can read the language in which it was written. This speed may be frightening for some in the book market. From there, it is easy to understand that they are tempted to recreate their usual business models in the digital book market in order to feel reassured. Through two fictitious examples, we will see on one hand, what would result from the temptation to repeat the old habits of the traditional book market in the virtual book market. On the other hand, we will imagine all the possibilities offered by the application of the specific logic of the virtual book market, and by the fact that it accelerates the circulation of information.

CHAPTER 4

Information scarcity or information abundance: the choices permitted by technological progress

We will take here the example of two fictitious States in two fictitious countries, which have hypothetically adopted an opposite approach to the emerging virtual book market. One is a State in a country of information affluence, which has benefited greatly from the possibilities offered by the Internet, digitalization of book and print-on-demand technologies. In the second country, which we have named the country of information scarcity, the State and the book industry have tried to replicate the old patterns of the printed book market within the virtual book market.

1: The option for information abundance

In the country in which information affluence is chosen, the law helps promote the circulation of books, and helps eliminate all kinds of censorship. Every author can be published. Digital versions of books are extremely cheap. The State has calculated that it is not profitable to levy sales taxes on digital books, because the technological equipment to do this would be costly, and an unconstitutional control over citizens would be implied. Moreover, this State has noticed that the increased circulation of digital books creates greater wealth in the tangible economic market. In this market, this State therefore knows how to levy taxes, which is easier to do in a tangible market that it can more easily control. Consequently, this State has decided to totally free the whole virtual publishing market from the burden of tax and tax law. In this country, all public budgets that could otherwise have been devoted to technological devices for the control of citizens and to fight tax evasion have instead been used to promote technologies that facilitate sales and provide a broader choice of books at a lower price. Given the extremely low price of digital books, payment systems have been set up that do not involve the mandatory identification of the buyer. These are prepaid cards and other means to preserve the anonymity of buyers and avoid the high commissions of banks on

Internet-based transactions. In this country, the owners of copyrighted works have well understood that they must count with readers if they wish to have their copyright respected by them. Instead of spending considerable amounts to have their digital books secured with expensive processes that will eventually be cracked, they have opted for selling their digital books (slightly secured) at extremely low prices. They also regularly campaign to encourage readers to respect copyrights, as it is the only way to maintain low prices on digital books and cultural abundance for all. In other words, in this country, readers are no longer interested in pirating books or in facilitating such piracy, because the price for legally acquiring a book is ridiculous compared to the risks incurred when infringing the law. While in other countries information technology companies are busy researching means to secure digital files so that they will not be easily cracked, in this country IT companies prefer to use their time and means in order to invent solutions to make digital books more attractive. In the country of information affluence, print-on-demand technologies are already widespread. This country is a haven (even fiscally) for authors worldwide who can be published here in either their native language or in the international language, and be almost instantaneously distributed through domestic and worldwide book channels. In this country, ideas flow faster than ever. The acceleration of the circulation of thought has boosted all the other branches of the economy and created many qualified jobs. The increased flow of ideas has given place to cultural abundance and high intellectual stimulation. All this has snowballed and created a prosperous economy. In this country there are no free e-books (apart from some exceptions) but there are no expensive e-books (apart from some exceptions). Almost all the books are available as e-books at a derisory price. The main consequence is that readers use libraries, not because they cannot or do not wish to buy expensive books, but for their pleasure. Most of the time the cost of transportation to the nearest library permits the purchase of one or several e-books without being trapped in traffic jams. Paradoxically, in this country libraries have many printed books, even though they no longer buy books. Indeed they receive free books from publishers and in exchange, they mention in their catalogue the existence of the e-book version and the link to buy them directly. The budgets of these libraries are almost exclusively devoted to other things than buying books. Some libraries act as virtual booksellers for books printed on demand. These books are not free, whereas access to the printed books on their shelves remains free for all. In this country, libraries play an important role in cultural animation and in helping localize intellectual resources throughout the world. They also act as the guardian of the collective memory of the humankind. Indeed in this country of information affluence, it has been decided that libraries would form a net to take charge of the storage of printed versions of books, so that if there is natural catastrophe, electricity problem or terrorist act, the country would not be deprived of its collective memory, which would otherwise be wiped out by the sudden bulk deletion of all electronic files, or the impossibility of accessing them. Moreover, librarians believe that storing printed books is better than "storing" copies of e-books, as this frees libraries from the constraints of technological changes that may render unusable e-books "stored" a long time previously. Libraries in this country also act as trustees for the provision of books and e-books to poor countries, and people who cannot afford even the low price of e-books or cannot yet access the technological devices to acquire them. One other major role of libraries consists of networking in order to set up worldwide catalogs of books available. In these catalogs, all available books are registered and authors and publishers have to pay nothing for this. To ensure that no knowledge is censored, their right to have their works listed in these catalogs is legally protected. It has become an important constitutional right. Indeed, this legal protection is important to this State, which has learnt lessons from the past where it was so easy for entities without counterpowers to block the advancement of science, culture and technology. In this generous and welcoming country of information affluence, books are now published in all languages and copyright laws have been modernized to reflect these changes. Authors need only make a virtual legal deposit of their works in order to have them identified and registered in databases of available books. The distribution channels of books in the country of information affluence are both domestic and worldwide. Catalogs of books are available in many languages. Information about e-books is gathered in all languages all over the world and books can be downloaded and printed on demand wherever readers wish. Inside this country all market practices are focused on promoting the increased circulation of books. For example, in this country, ink cartridges are exceptionally cheap. Meanwhile, in other countries their price does not encourage readers - who do not like reading on electronic devices - to buy e-books that, once printed, would cost them more than books sold which are already printed. In these countries, the seller of printing devices, instead of investing in devices to avoid refilling cartridges, have ended up in investing in print-on-demand technologies and in selling books printed on demand. In the country of information affluence, people can buy books almost everywhere, and not only at bookstores - for example, at the hairdresser's, where before only tabloids were available to them, customers can now access a virtual library and have the book of their choice printed on demand or downloaded onto their e-book reader device. The fact that in the country of information affluence, the market is open to all authors, national or foreign, has stimulated many aspects of cultural life. Innovation in all fields has been boosted by new ideas from abroad and by the elimination of disguised censorship that had still existed, mainly in universities and research centers. The prosperity created by the expansion of the virtual book market has permitted the creation of many new research centers, schools and universities, where in turn jobs for more and more researchers have been created. In these research centers, many teams have worked on understanding the brain's processes of creativity, in an atmosphere of intellectual freedom. Fundamental discoveries have been made and the inventors of the country have been granted an incredibly high number of patents in all the key fields of research. The State is finally extremely satisfied with its choice of a policy of tax exemption in the virtual book market. Such a policy has permitted the virtual book market to take off and to generate in other fields much greater tax incomes than what the State could have hoped from a poorer virtual book market hampered by state taxes, banks fees, etc... Thanks to this policy, all authors are exempt from taxation on the royalties they receive, while they are allowed to deduct from other incomes the expenses they have incurred in order to make their work available to the book market. In this country, there is no longer any need to subsidize non-commercial books, as it is so cheap to publish new books that everybody can express new ideas, even in niche markets. Moreover, the book market has become the most prosperous market in the country, also due the fact that many other countries have adopted a policy of scarcity. Obviously, time was needed to achieve all these good results, and a change in the reader mentality was necessary in order for readers to understand that respecting copyright is in their own interest. Time was also needed to suppress every kind of censorship, apparent or disguised, that still existed in this liberal country. From time to time, the country of information affluence was confronted with some crisis: huge power failures that led the State to imagine other energy strategies. Terrorist attacks on information technologies that led to decentralization and networking, instead of concentration. All research centers have been solicited to imagine new strategies to better solve all of these problems. Finally, the policy of the State in the country of information affluence has permitted unprecedented human, economic and social progress, to such an extent that a sizeable intellectual, social and economic gap now exists between the country of information affluence and the country of information scarcity which is far from having known such an evolution. In the meanwhile, what has happened there?

2: The option for information scarcity

In the country of information scarcity, the decision to adopt a policy of scarcity is taken mainly because it advantageous for some economic agents. These agents believe they have no interest in changing the business models of the book market. Consequently, they try to repeat into the virtual market all of the conditions that, in the traditional book market, made possible their power to control the market, the flow of ideas and the entry of new competitors. These economic agents are supported by the State, which like them has an interest in controlling the flow of digital books. The State wants to levy taxes on e-books and uses every possible means available to control the flow of digital books and to levy taxes automatically. The heavy burden of bureaucracy is added to this context. In fact, in this country the flow of e-books is considerably hindered by material, administrative and psychological obstacles. In this country, print-on-demand technologies do not allow, as is the case in the country of information affluence, the publication of many new authors. This is due to two main reasons: one related to tax law, the other to the policy of information scarcity. Contrary to the country of information affluence which was a tax haven for authors, in the country of scarcity the tax law is absolutely deterrent for small businesses, and published and self-published authors are considered small businesses. Moreover, self-published authors must pay high amounts in taxes, even if they lose money in their venture. Due to this hostile tax system, in this country, setting up a small publishing company to sell e-books or to use print-on-demand technologies remains a risky activity. (In the country of information affluence, anyone could do this at almost no risk). Despite the burden of this tax system, new publishing companies are nevertheless created thanks to print-on-demand technologies. Unfortunately, they have the idea to take advantage of the imbalance between supply (many authors) and demand (the small number of books permitted to enter the book market) to pass obviously imbalanced agreements with new authors and to continue excluding many of them. Finally, in this country, instead of contributing to opening the market to many new authors, print-on-demand technologies have made the situation of many authors even worse than before, as they have invested money to publish their book but cannot enter the distribution channels reserved for traditional publishers. (Conversely, in the country of information affluence, these distribution channels are open to all). In the country of information scarcity, a centralized national database of books available for sale is under the control of the book industry, which does not allow registration of self-published works or works published through print-on-demand technologies. (Whereas in the country of information affluence all books are registered in the business databases of books available for sale). In other words, in the country of information scarcity, despite technological progress, registration of new books in professional databases is reserved, as in the past, to traditional publishers who use offset printing and stock large quantities of books. In addition to being barred from registration in book industry catalogs, books published or self-published using print-on-demand technologies are rejected even by the National Library in charge of the legal deposit of books. Due to this situation, for booksellers and for readers it is as if books printed on demand do not exist. In the country of scarcity, despite the progress of communication technology, ideas do not circulate easily. Books printed-on-demand and e-books exist on the fringes of the book market and technological progress has had almost no impact on the book industry. Publishers continue to do as before: they publish a narrow range of commercial books as well as some non-commercial books subsidized by the State. Both market censorship and censorship from universities is hard on authors. And the elite of research bars many innovative authors from being published. In the country of scarcity, the price of books, even of e-books, is abnormally high. This leads to a high level of piracy of copyrighted works by those who are disrespectful to the system. The digital book market does not succeed and piracy is high in spite of DRM technologies and criminal laws supposed to be deter it. In this country, because public libraries are poor in books and no longer free, the "black market" for pirated e-books and the second-hand market for books both flourish and huge expenses are incurred by the book industry to unsuccessfully combat piracy and copyright infringements. On another side, the way technology is used in order to control citizen has put the State itself in danger. Indeed, it would be possible for hackers to control citizens, instead of the State! Hence this leads to a vicious circle of ever-increasing control on people. Security of technology is of major concern for the

State in the country of scarcity. Here, huge amounts are spent in securing technical means used to control citizens and to levy taxes online. Despite this heavy atmosphere, the *status quo* is maintained for a while without major problems for the book industry. People continue to buy expensive commercial books because they have no choice. Libraries that are relatively poor are nevertheless full of people, as many readers do not want to pay or cannot afford the high price of books. The book industry has lobbied the government to legally rule against the free lending of books by libraries, but readers have devised many ways to circumvent this law.

In spite of all this, the country of scarcity can continue with this policy because the domestic market is still captive, as people in this country do not read in other languages and other countries generally do not publish in their language, and when they do so they are unable to enter the well-protected domestic book market. But in the course of time, the situation changes to the detriment of the country of scarcity and all gets bad very quickly. First, the book industry pays for the consequences of its policy of creation of artificial scarcity. This is because many authors of this country rejected by the traditional book market have in the meantime been published in the country of information abundance without even leaving their own country. These authors are many, as in the country of scarcity the conjunction of unemployment and high level of education leads people to writing a lot of books. With unemployment wages provided by the State, thinking and writing is the most affordable hobby. In this country there is a multitude of authors rejected by the book industry, whereas they are welcomed in the country of information affluence. Thanks to print-on-demand technologies and the Internet, this country now publishes all the authors in all languages and in the international language and distributes them worldwide. Thanks to the technological progress, the country of information affluence no longer needs to be physically on the territory of the country of scarcity to invade its book market. Moreover, the citizens of the country of scarcity have learned to read in the international language, because books in this language are cheaper, the choice is greater and they can find challenging books in many fields that cannot exist in their own country. Finally, the country of scarcity completely loses its ability to control the circulation of printed books on its own territory, due to the net of print-on-demand machines now existing on its territory and the impossibility of controlling the flow of ideas on the Internet. The entire wealth created by its own people has been diverted to the benefit of the country of information affluence. The book market of the country of scarcity cannot compete with foreign production in its own language, which is cheaper, more diverse and more interesting. The country of scarcity, which did not take advantage of the new communication technologies, has taken a considerable intellectual and technological step backwards. Moreover, every hacker of this country has helped the country of information affluence to culturally invade the country of scarcity. The biggest concern is now the gap that has been created within a short time between the country of scarcity and the country of abundance. The country of scarcity is now an underdeveloped country, compared to the country of information affluence, having gradually lost its authors, designers, computer engineers, artists, translators and researchers who could not find employment in their own country, or who preferred the more stimulating atmosphere of the country of information affluence. Among those authors excluded by the commercial book market and by the elite for the subsidized book market are the country's most original and interesting people. All their competences, useless in their own country, have been welcomed in the country of information affluence. Thanks to this flow of new ideas, the gap between the country of scarcity and the country of abundance has become definitive: the number of patents granted in the country of information affluence has exploded. Each year the country of information scarcity publishes a number of "new" books, which is ridiculous when compared with the high number of books published in the country of information affluence. In the country of information affluence, many universities, research centers and institutes have been created, which attract researchers and students from all countries. The country of information affluence has made considerable progress in many fields, thanks to the diversion to its advantage of all the flow of ideas that are considered useless in other countries. The country of information affluence dominates in all fields of human knowledge and has <u>unrivalled</u> power to decide the intellectual future of humankind and to manage its cultural heritage.

The two examples we have taken are obviously fictitious and exaggerated, but we can draw from them many lessons.

CHAPTER 5

Lessons we can draw from these examples and other observations on the transformation of publishing

1: The option for information scarcity is a dead end for all

The virtual world and the physical world do not obey the same laws of functioning. If in the physical world the option for information scarcity may appear beneficial, it is the opposite in a virtual context, where this option for scarcity leads to a dead end. Due to the specific manner in which the virtual economy works, an artificial creation of scarcity will quickly become detrimental to those who have opted for this. In a previous book about Internet Law, we have given the example of the French Minitel[15] (the first domestic French network) to demonstrate that the misuse of modern technology in order to create an artificial information scarcity is economically, technologically and socially harmful.

In the case of the Minitel, centralized control of the net allowed the use of this technology contrary to its purpose, which was to democratize access to information. With the misuse of Minitel, which created a scarcity of information, France forfeited any technological and social edge it could have gained from the Minitel, which at the time was a vanguard technology. The misuse of the Minitel did not favor its technological improvement. It quickly became obsolete and was rapidly overtaken by the Internet. Today, DRM software tends to be used by copyright holders to maintain relatively high prices for e-books and maintain strict controls on readers. From this perspective, is it not surprising that the e-book market has not succeeded. Instead, it would be better to seize the opportunities offered by the technology to create an abundance of e-books for all, priced as low as possible, with as much freedom of use for readers as possible. Using the technology this way would accelerate the circulation of ideas and books, both digital and printed on demand, or traditionally. The informational abundance expected from technological progress has not yet taken place. Instead, the observation of the book market shows that the book industry tends to recreate the distribution models of the printed book market in the virtual book market. This is why we find wholesalers, distributors, booksellers and so on in the virtual market. Some wholesalers of e-books have managed to accumulate huge databases of e-books, made possible thanks to the high price of DRM technologies that many publishers cannot afford. In this case, publishers have passed a distribution agreement with the wholesaler, who in turn has licensed the right to sell the e-books to virtual booksellers. Generally, small publishers cannot even afford to buy the right to sell their own protected e-books! The trade discount for the e-books wholesaler is generally the same as the trade discount for traditional printed books (up to 55%). Most of the time, due to the prohibitive cost of DRM technologies, in regard to the small quantities of e-books that are expected to sell in the present state of the book market, publishers cannot afford DRM software and consequently cannot sell their own e-books.

The transposition of business models of the printed book market to the virtual market was made necessary artificially by the need to protect digital files and the prohibitive cost of DRM technologies. In other words, technological advances that otherwise could have been used to free the flow of e-books and to get rid of the traditional business models (necessary for books as objects but useless for e-books) have been used to do the opposite. Subsequently the e-book market does not succeed and nobody benefits from the technological advances as readers continue to buy printed books in the traditional way! The e-book market will never take off if e-books remain expensive. For now they are expensive solely due to trade discounts paid which are similar to those in the traditional business model: online banking fees, and in some countries sales taxes or VAT as high as 19.6% in France! For all these reasons e-books cannot be sold at low prices and the e-books market cannot gain a foothold. Neither the book industry nor readers benefit from the information affluence that, with a more appropriate use of new communication technologies and a more generous attitude of States and of the book industry, could have been made possible. Instead this technology has been used to create scarcity: expensive e-books allowing little freedom of use to the end reader, prohibitive DRM software many publishers cannot afford, and in some countries incredibly greedy sales taxes that are almost four times higher than the same taxes on printed books!

2: The globalization of the book market involves a change of approach to this market

Contrary to what some believe, the Internet will not bring about the end of the respect of the author's right and of the book industry. New communication technologies and the Internet are only tools that we can use as we wish. At this point, we need to widen the approach to the book market if we want to benefit from the technological progress. Even if books need a market and its laws to circulate, we must not limit our thinking to that market alone. Instead, we must adopt a comprehensive approach to publishing. The many projects of universal libraries,[16] elaborated from Antiquity until the present day with the Google Books project, show the ever-lasting role played by books as keepers of the collective memory. As part of the chain of this collective memory, we find many different characters:

authors, publishers, libraries, booksellers and also readers, who also contribute to the circulation of ideas and to the life of this collective memory. Through the circulation of ideas transformed into written words in books or e-books, it is life itself that circulates. Every link of the book circulation chain is necessary for the correct flow of ideas and everybody, from author to end reader, must be taken into account in the creation of a prosperous modern book market.[17] If any of these links in the book market is neglected, this slows down the circulation of ideas. For example, if authors are not paid for their work, they may stop writing and the spring of creation will cease. If readers cannot afford to buy books, or do not want to do so, then there is no market possible. In this case, it is not only the book industry that suffers from this situation, but also all intellectual and cultural life of humankind for lack of stimulation. When governments secure the right of authors to be paid for their work by giving them a legal monopoly on their work, they contribute to the circulation of ideas.[18] And the best protection of authors' rights is the public's respect for them and its will to give them something in exchange for their works. Unfortunately, despite communication campaigns encouraging people to respect copyrights, too many copyrighted works continue to be pirated. Hence the circle of exchanges - crucial for a healthy book market and a good circulation of information – is broken, which raises the argument that the price to pay for books is too high. The use of new technologies should improve this situation by making books available at low prices in digital format. This does not prevent the printed books industry (traditionally printed or on demand) from existing in its own right. When e-books actually become inexpensive, there will be little interest in going to a library to photocopy a book, to borrowing a book from a friend and even using second-hand books. Readers will no longer be concerned with infringing copyrights.[19] Contrary to what some authors believe, the use of technology to protect the copyrighted works is not the most efficient way to protect them. The history of information technology has shown how quickly new technology can be cracked and how much hackers can take pleasure in infringing these codes.[20] Such use of technology in order to protect copyrighted works and to dictate the way the end user is able to read e-books is similar to the French public's approach to Minitel. We have already explained[21] what happened in France with

Minitel, how it was misused, and how France forfeited all the benefits of this vanguard technology. Let us not make the same mistake with new communication technologies. The law of scarcity may work in the tangible economy, but in a virtual market, this logic does not work at all. We can do much better with a logic of abundance. The following assertion, found in a report issued in France, shows that the logic of the virtual market has not been understood. This assertion is wrong in the virtual book market and we should discard it absolutely if we want to create a prosperous book market:

> "Economy exists only when there is scarcity and people are attracted by this scarcity. We should set up (in the digital market) technical solutions to create scarcity".[22]

Limitation and scarcity are the laws of a material world, whereas abundance and lack of restrictions are the laws of a virtual world. Why should we use software to recreate the problems of the material world in the virtual world? Nobody will benefit from this scarcity and we will all forfeit the advantages of a virtual economy. For the first time in our history, we have the technology to create a wealthy and generous virtual book market. If e-books are sold at low prices, authors and publishers will be financially rewarded for the many sales that would not otherwise exist. People will also continue buying printed books, and chances are that popular e-books will be also sold in printed versions.[23] In many cases, e-books sold at extremely low prices will serve the same kind of way as the "search inside the book" function currently available on Amazon and other online booksellers. Publishers could also adopt a distribution strategy of e-books in partnership with public libraries. They could, for example, give printed books to libraries for free, while in exchange libraries would list the e-book version in their catalogs and set up links to buy them. This would be an affordable marketing option for niche and small publishing companies. With e-books sold at a low cost, everybody would be satisfied and the book market would be boosted. On the contrary, maintaining artificial scarcity in the virtual book market (through high priced e-books) will only encourage piracy of copyrighted works, prevent progression in the book industry and ultimately be harmful to all. In the book industry's present context, it is also important that the e-book stay subject to the law of exchange. In other words, e-books should not be free, and we are going to explain why.

3: Providing books for free would be prejudicial to a correct circulation of ideas

Contrary to what James J. O'DONNELL believes, in the future books must not be free[24] (they may be free only in exceptional cases), because this would break the circle of exchanges and slow down the circulation of ideas. In such a scenario, who would continue writing? Probably rich people, scholars, religious people, civil officers and some individuals sponsored by large companies. We would return to a situation equivalent to the situation of authors long before the Revolution in France: no actual rights for authors and a situation which makes it easy for States to control ideas and their flow. It would be a regrettable drawback as history has shown that entities such as universities, churches and States, while they have contributed on one hand to preserve human knowledge, have also on the other hand eliminated disturbing works and occasionally the authors as well. Nowadays censorship still exists, even in the most liberal of countries, and many innovative ideas are barred from the book market. In the context of a virtual worldwide book market, censorship added to the artificial creation of scarcity would no longer work. Moreover it would be suicidal for a country.

The important conclusion to draw from this first part is that it is necessary to use new communication technology in accordance with its purpose, that is, to accelerate the circulation of ideas. This is the only winning option for the increasingly global book market. In order to achieve this aim, the book market needs a more appropriate and stimulating legal framework.

In the second part of this book we will examine which legal concepts should be revised and what should be the guidelines to modernize copyright law, so that it can favor positive changes in the book market.

PART 2

LEGAL PROPOSALS

TO HELP DEVELOP

THE VIRTUAL BOOK MARKET

We have seen in the first part that the dominant legal philosophy does not allow lawyers to depart from positive law (i.e. the set of existing texts) and to look at the changing reality of publishing. From this fact, the philosophy of law has produced no thinking that could help the modernization of copyright law, so that it could in turn help the development of the book market. Despite the extent of the changes within the publishing industry, most of the time lawyers continue to study and comment on their old texts, without being aware of how much some deep-rooted legal concepts are ill-adapted to a virtual book market. In the following chapters we will see current legal practices in the field of copyright. We will then explain why some concepts such as intellectual property, or the traditional idea of justice, are not suited to the virtual world, and we will propose more appropriate legal solutions.

CHAPTER 1

The *status quo* in the field of copyright law

In a recent interview, John Perry BARLOW asserted that the modern world does not know how the virtual economy of information works. In the field of law, this is manifest by the will of lawyers and economic agents attempting to transpose legal and social practices that were created for a physical world to the virtual world, and focused on the concept of property. In modern law, literary and artistic works are objects of property and we try to protect them the way we protect other properties, using power, violence, prohibition, electronic devices against theft and so on. From this, as they now stand, copyright laws are helping economic agents wishing to create the information scarcity of the printed book market in the virtual book market. Instead, copyright law should be creatively modernized in order to aid the most advantageous use of the Internet and new communication technology. We have seen how harmful to all the creation of an artificial scarcity in the virtual world has become. Due to the fact that copyright laws are focused on tangible objects and centered on the concept of property, they have become more and more complex, coercive, intrusive, numerous, and at the same time, inefficient - to such an extent that a scholar specialist of copyright law was discouraged by the complexity of copyright laws.[25] Continental lawyers are finding it more and more difficult to deal with the many laws that have become so complex. Governmental bodies throughout the world are acting without a comprehensive approach to the virtual economy and under the hard pressure of the large companies involved in the market of copyrighted works like books, movies and music. It is clear from the present situation that an in-depth reflection on the legal nature of author's rights and a comprehensive approach to the virtual economy are lacking. We can also see that the important cultural choice that should be made collectively is imposed by a small number of people wanting to use the communication technology in a manner contrary to its purpose. In other words, while communication technologies are deemed to favor the circulation speed of information, these economic agents are trying to use them in order to control the information flow, and in so doing to recreate in the virtual book market the information scarcity of the printed book market. As we have already mentioned, the virtual economy does not obey the same laws as the physical economy. Indeed, the virtual economy is characterized by abundance, whereas the material economy is marked by scarcity and by the law of supply and demand. Due to this fundamental difference, our traditional idea of justice is not suited to the virtual book market and a more appropriate concept of justice is necessary.

CHAPTER 2

The traditional concept of justice is unsuited to the virtual book market

1: The art of Justice as the root of law

The art of justice is no longer studied by modern lawyers, who consider justice to be outside of the sphere of law. For example, according to the famous legal philosopher Hans KELSEN, a leading figure of legal positivism, justice should be excluded from the science of law. To him, such a concept pertains to the field of emotions and must be excluded, in order to allow only a rational and objective approach to the Law.[26] However, without a previous human need of justice, we would never have had any legal rules, and legal positivism would have never existed. But we tend to forget that justice has preceded law, because as lawyers we are so used to dealing with laws. Codes and laws are only the consequences of the art of justice. Without the will to render justice, law would never have existed. The role of the written law is to facilitate justice, but the law in itself is not the art of justice. The actual art of justice does not consist of knowing and applying old inappropriate texts to unprecedented situations, but it does consist of creating pragmatic solutions to balance relations between people when a new problem arises. In other words, the actual art of justice consists in finding what is just and in creating intelligent solutions to new problems, instead of asking only whether a pre-existing set of laws should apply to a new situation, or if we are faced with a legal void. Without an initial longing for justice, the law as we know it would never have existed. Written laws are only the materialization of innovative legal solutions found in the past through the art of justice. This is why, when drastic changes take place in a field of human activities, as is the case today in publishing, the shorter way to find appropriate rules for this emerging market is to determine what is justice in this new context, and not which old set of laws should be applied or amended. In other words, the most direct way of finding solutions to the new legal

70

problems raised by the virtual book market is to go to the root and ask what is justice in this new context. This is much more useful than asking: Is this paragraph of copyright law applicable? Is copyright better that continental authors' right? How can we protect the authors' property? It would be better to go to the root and ask: What is justice in the virtual book market? Which concept of justice should apply? What should be the aim of justice in the virtual book market? What is the fairest way to use new communication technologies? Once we have defined justice in a virtual context, it is then much easier to create the law because we know the way to be followed and the aim to be achieved. At this point old laws, which may prove useful in this new context, may also be used to regulate the new context. So, let us think about what justice is in the virtual book market.

2: Justice in the virtual and in the physical worlds

In the traditional world, justice is seen as the art of sharing material goods and honors existing in a limited amount and in punishing infringers of the law. This kind of

71

justice, which gives to each its own, is well suited to a world where goods and honors exist in a limited number. It is easily understandable that a world of scarcity has given birth to a philosophy of justice made for a world of scarcity. In this world, justice is not creative; its aim is to share only what already exists. In other words, justice is used to balance the relationships between people regarding things that exist in a limited amount. In the virtual world, generally speaking, there is no longer scarcity. The virtual world is the domain of abundance, where giving something to someone does not deprive the donor, as it is the case in the material world. In the virtual world, an idea can be communicated to many people without depriving its inventor. In the material world, the more we receive, the richer we become; in the virtual world the more we communicate the more opportunities we have to enrich ourselves intellectually and also

72

materially. Intangibility equals unlimited abundance. In a virtual world where things exist in an unlimited amount, a justice consisting mainly of sharing scarcity is no longer useful and we must think about a new concept of justice. As has already been explained in detail in a previous book about Internet law, justice in the virtual world is different from the justice we know in the traditional world.[27] Justice can be much better than a distributive justice alone, it can be creative, generating abundance. In a virtual context, justice should be not the art of sharing scarcity, which does not exist, but the art of creating maximum abundance for all, thanks to the acceleration of the circulation of the information flow. All that favors the circulation of ideas in the virtual world is just, given that increased circulation of ideas leads to increased wealth. By the same token, all that blocks or slows down the circulation of ideas is unfair in the virtual world. And one important thing must be kept in mind: the virtual market is global; therefore justice in the virtual market is global too. This is not the case in the traditional market, where justice as the art of sharing applies within well-delimited domestic territories. This means that, in the material world, when a State is just and allows the people to live in a just country, this has no important consequences for neighboring countries. In the same line, injustice can also be limited to a country without important consequences for its neighboring countries and the rest of the world. This is no longer the case in the virtual world, where everything is global, even justice. There, indeed justice (=free flow of ideas) in one country or injustice (obstruction to the flow of ideas) in another country has important consequences for all other countries linked to the Internet. One fundamental law of the cyberspace is that an unfair State (i.e. a State that tries to slow down or to obstruct the circulation of information on its own territory) automatically transfers the flow of wealth that follows the flow of ideas to other countries more favorable to justice (in the meaning of the virtual world that is to say States who favor the circulation of ideas). In the virtual world, the injustice of a State quickly turns against it. We have already seen how it may occur through the example we have taken of the State which opted for the creation of information scarcity. This country, as we have seen, unlike the country of information affluence - where new communication technologies are used to create information abundance - has an unfair attitude when it comes to trying to recreate the scarcity of the material world in the virtual world. As a result of this, this country could not benefit from the creation of wealth engendered by the acceleration of the information flow. Having now determined what justice is in the virtual world, let us now see why the circulation of ideas brings prosperity.

3: Virtual justice=increased information flow and increased wealth in all fields

Modern economic analysis has clearly shown that the increase in information flow leads to higher physical wealth.[28] We have seen how the Internet has been beneficial to economies throughout the world and particularly to the American economy.[29] There, Bill GATES declared to company managers: "Information flow is your lifeblood."[30] History makes obvious that increases in the circulation of ideas have been the main driving force behind the evolution of our civilization. The invention of the printing press by GUTENBERG, through lowering the price of books increased the speed of circulation of ideas, as well as the social and cultural development of the Western world. Nowadays, the Internet and new publishing technologies allow the considerable improvement of the economy of the book market. This market is still hindered by many obstacles: [31] physical, economic, psychological, administrative or

76

linguistic, which slow down or block the "flow of books". If we use them correctly, the Internet and the new communication technologies will allow us to eliminate many of the traditional obstacles that block the circulation of books, which should lead to considerable expansion of the book market. Such an acceleration of the flow of books can only lead to unprecedented global prosperity, as economists believe that: "Disseminating ideas is desirable and necessary for the prosperity of a society."[32] It is now clear that, in the context of the virtual book market, Justice does not consist of sharing a scarcity that does not exist, but in creating information affluence for all. In order that this kind of justice can be set up, it is necessary to revise other fundamental legal concepts that are unsuited to the virtual book market. Among them, the concept of intellectual property is a major handicap to the necessary modernization of copyright law and to a different approach to the economy of the virtual book market.

CHAPTER 3

The concept of intellectual property unsuited to the virtual book market

In this chapter, we will ask if in a general manner the right of an author can be considered a right of property. We have seen in chapter two, dedicated to the definition of books, that printed books are means to materializing intangible thought. Therefore the essential nature of a book is to be a message, that is to say an intangible object that cannot be owned the way we own tangible objects. The laws of physics do not make ownership of intangible things possible. So why do lawyers speak of intellectual property?

1: Is it legally possible to own an intangible idea the same way we own physical objects?

When books circulate on the Internet as intangible e-books, we can understand how impossible it is to deal with physically intangible things. Contrary to what is asserted in many copyright laws, the laws of nature make ownership of intangible items like ideas impossible. From there, the right of property, which was initially applied to material objects only, is not appropriate for literary works made of intangible ideas. And Geoffrey BROWN is right in his assertion:

> "Many of the difficulties encountered in talking about rights over information spring from the concepts of property and ownership..."[33]

Nowadays, the legal concept of intellectual property is so common that nobody thinks about challenging it. This should be done, as the concept of intellectual property has become one of the major obstacles to efficient copyright law. Generally, modern books on copyright law are entitled "Intellectual property Law" or "Copyright Law". Most of the time, they just ignore philosophy of law or legal theory. They just list all the modern domestic laws and international agreements in the field and comment on them, then they compare the US copyright system to the continental system. Throughout the world, all copyright laws, domestic as well as international, tend to be emptier and emptier of philosophical legal thinking. And a law deprived from philosophy cannot evolve when dramatic changes occur in reality. This is why copyright laws worldwide are no longer suited to the modern publishing world. In the best cases, books on copyright law briefly expose the history of copyright law, but never challenge the concept of intellectual property. When Mark ROSE rightly asserts:

> "Many jurists have been aware of the awkwardness of treating literary texts as private property. Nevertheless, the institution of the literary property is so deeply rooted in our society that many jurists and even some legal historians regard it as a transcendent moral idea that has been available in all times and places."[34]

He merely states a reality that has been made compulsory due to the "pure theory of law", that is to say legal positivism, which confines lawyers to the study and the application of positive law (i.e. the existing set of laws). In many countries, legal positivism has become obligatory for lawyers, scholars and law students, so that when they adopt a different approach to law, the establishment bars them from everywhere it can. For lack of counter power, this drastic censorship occurs in the most liberal countries to the detriment of society, which cannot benefit from innovative thinkers in the field of law. As for legal practice, every practitioner's mind is shaped by this philosophy, which is the background for all modern legal teaching. As Michel VILLEY asserts, they are positivists without even being aware of it. In consequence, criticism on the concept of intellectual property will not be found in legal doctrine, but in other fields such as Economy. Some economists have indeed observed that, pragmatically speaking, the concept of property is not suited to the intellectual context. Having analyzed copyright law, they conclude:

> "It is important to recognize that, economically speaking, intellectual properties are not properties – as tangible commodities - despite the misleading term, and intellectual property laws do not protect the said property, but the interests of the owners derived from the use of that property – although this interest may very well be termed as "property" in the legal sense."[35]

Another author underlines the oddity of the concept of intellectual property as follows:

> "It ought to be obvious that there is something odd about the use of the concept of ownership in this context. Information considering simply as such is by

82

no means the kind of thing that can be owned, though as we shall see it can sometimes be bought and sold."

Of course, despite the assertion of law, natural laws do not make possible the ownership of an idea, because ideas are not tangible. So, why, against common sense, can we find in positive law and even in recent books on Internet Law or copyright law, the assertion that the right of authors is a right of property? [36]

Nowadays, dogmatic discussion of the nature of authors' rights is no longer fashionable. It seems useless to modern lawyers who are content with the study of positive law. Contrary to contemporary lawyers, those who in 1886 drafted the Bern Convention, were particularly interested in this subject. Lively discussions on the topic took place, but due to the lack of unanimity on the nature of these rights, lawyers eventually stopped discussing this issue as it was deemed too complex and sterile. Long before them, this question fascinated the world and had been discussed by philosophers, lawyers and politicians who invented a multitude of theories on the subject.[37] Pierre RECHT has presented all these theories in an interesting book on copyright law.[38] In his book, Pierre RECHT observes that the European ideological disagreement on the nature of authors' rights did not get in the way of reaching an agreement on the practical measures to be adopted in the framework of the Bern convention.[39] In the same sense, as recently as 1908, Eugène POUILLET, who was favorable to the Intellectual property doctrine, believed that these doctrinal debates were not so important. He wrote:

> "Let us first observe that the question is purely theoretical and that nobody thinks about depriving authors from a right on their works. The problem is only to know how we will name this right and the disagreement stands mainly in the vocabulary that should be used. To the contrary, in practice it is not important to state that this right is a right of property as long as the effects, the extent and the duration of this right is clearly determined by the law."[40]

Throughout History, it is easy to understand why doctrinal disputes about the nature of authors' rights stopped. The époque's need for practicality was enough to solve the problem encountered in the field. Today, the important changes taking place into the book market make it necessary to clearly understand the legal category of authors' right.

The concept of intellectual property, so useful long ago, must now be challenged, for it is unsuited to the new economic world of publishing. Such a concept is today a major obstacle to clear formulation of the problems and to attaining efficient modernization of a copyright law adapted to reality. The concept of intellectual property is totally unreal. In fact, it is a legal fiction, as we say in legal jargon. And it is interesting to understand why this legal fiction was created.

2: The genesis of the concept of intellectual property

World History, the history of the French Revolution especially, clearly shows how the concept of intellectual property was born.[41] If it is today admitted that authors must receive a portion of the benefits drawn through the sale of their works,[42] this has not been always the case. To achieve this progress, mentalities had to evolve, authors had to fight, and the book market had to expand.[43] Gradually, royal authorities began granting privileges on the sales of books to booksellers and later on, to authors directly. It is only from the beginning of the 18th century that privileges were granted directly to authors.[44] Before that, they were granted only to booksellers.[45] As we can see, authors' rights in the beginning were not rights of property but privileges. Being privileges implies that these rights pertain to the category of personal rights, instead of the category of real rights (real in the legal meaning means "material" it comes from the Latin "res" which means material thing). Personal rights, contrary to real rights, are focused on people and not on material objects. The legal category of personal rights deals with personal relationships. According to Mark ROSE, in England the London booksellers first used the concept of intellectual property in order to transform temporary privileges into privileges, permanent like property. In France before the Revolution, authors had no right of intellectual property, but privileges. French history clearly shows why and how the author's privileges were transformed into rights of property. In France, during the night of August 4, 1789, revolutionaries abolished all the existing privileges granted by royal authorities in many fields.[46] Due to this abolition, authors' privileges were also deemed to disappear along with inventors' privileges. But creators' privileges were considered too useful to be suppressed, and revolutionaries found a solution for keeping them

86

alive despite the abolition of all privileges. The psychological context prevented them from using the word "privilege", which was considered too tainted by royal abuses, but encouraged them to use the concept of property, which at this time was greatly valued by philosophers and people.[47] The French revolutionaries saved the authors' and inventors' privileges through fictitiously transforming them into rights of property.[48] They were inspired by the French, English and American legal doctrine of this time.[49]

This law came into effect during the vote of the French decrees of January 13-19, 1791 and July 19-24, 1793, which granted property rights to authors. At this time, with property at the top of the political, philosophical and social agendas, it was the most apt legal concept for saving the privileges of the authors. This kind of magical trick was so successful that, later on, it paved the way for the concept of incorporeal or intangible property that still exists in the French Code of Intellectual Property.[50] The belief of Pierre BOURDIEU that: "The most rational law is merely an act of social magic that is successful", can be fully verified in this historical example.[51] Through the use of the word "property" instead of "privileges", the revolutionaries could save the ancient privileges of the French authors. They also strengthened authors' legal status, thanks to an efficient, well-conceived law which lasted more than 160 years without any major amendments, despite the fiction of property.[52]

The study of the world history of copyright law shows how difficult it has been in a materialist civilization to protect the intangible wealth of intellectual creativity. It was necessary, in order to achieve a deserved legal protection, to use the category of the right of property, instead of the category of personal rights. In the 18th century, the fiction of intellectual property was necessary to maintain and strengthen the authors' legal statute. Today this fiction is no longer necessary, moreover, it is harmful to a sound reflection about the modernization of copyright law, and it would be better to discard it. Despite its negative aspects, the concept of privilege proves that the rights granted to authors by the kings where personal rights. In fact, even under the right of property label, the authors' rights have never ceased to be in reality a personal right. Today, it would be useful to recognize this simple reality.

CHAPTER 4

The actual nature of authors' rights, its importance in the creation of an efficient copyright law

Through granting a privilege to an author, the King gave this author the legal power to act upon other people, in order to prevent people from performing any actions parasitic to the author's work. In France, without the Revolution, the rights of authors might naturally have ended up being personal rights.[53] The problem is not rewriting history, but to be aware that once the concept of property was useful, but now it is harmful. One of the major inconveniences of this concept is that minds have been for too long focused on the supposed "objects" of this property instead of being focused on people and on balancing their relationships in this context. To illustrate this fact, we quote Mark ROSE, who has written in an article entitled: "The Author as Proprietor":

"What we here observe, I would suggest, is a twin birth, the simultaneous emergence in the discourse of the law of the proprietary author and the literary work. The two concepts are bound to each other. to assert one is to imply the other, and together...they define the centre of the modern literary system."[54]

The author being a proprietor, the law seeks to protect this property the same way as other properties. Copyright laws are all so focused on these "objects" of property that they have forgotten the people. In a previous publication, we explained in detail the ancient Roman root of the modern distinction between real rights (real comes from the Latin res and in the legal context means: physical, material things and the right of property is a real right) and personal rights. We have shown in this study that whenever the law is confronted with the intangible world, in our case ideas, it is in fact confronted with people and has to use the category of personal rights and not the one of real rights (which was conceived for the tangible world). When confronted with the intangible world, for example innovative ideas or literary works, the law can only rely on people to manage this field, because physical control over the intangible world is impossible. In other words, lawyers can only rely on people when facing a

92

problem in the intangible world, as they cannot use the natural means we use to protect tangible objects that can be seized. In the 18th century, KANT[55] believed that authors' rights were personal rights. To him, the right of an author was a personal right, through which an author authorized a publisher to speak to the public on his behalf. It is now time to recognize the true nature of authors' rights. This way we will focus our minds, not on objects that do no longer exist in a virtual reality, but on persons and the balance of their relationship in the book market. The best way to find a solution to the new problems raised by technological changes in the field of publishing is to seek to balance relationships among people. Such an approach broadens the very narrow scope of the intellectual property approach. Thanks to a more comprehensive approach to the publishing industry, it allows us to imagine legal strategies capable of creating prosperity for each link of the book chain, from the author to the reader.[56] Let us change the approach to copyright law: instead of focusing the law on the supposed objects of a property right, let us instead look at people, their relationships in this area, their psychology, their general attitude. If we take into account the behavior of people

93

and their psychology, we will be able to channel their behavior with appropriate legal, technological and economic strategies. Technologies such as the Internet, e-books or DRM software are only technologies. We can use them to accelerate the flow of "books" and ideas. As Mark STEFIK[57] and Lawrence LESSIG[58] have shown, we can also use them to master, control and therefore slow down the circulation of ideas.

CHAPTER 5

Guidelines for the modernization of copyright law

1: The concept of intellectual property must be abandoned

The Internet, combined with print-on-demand technology, new e-book reader devices, and DRM software, has brought the possibilities to create a much wealthier book market than the one we know, as well as information affluence for all, and income for many more authors. We simply have to decide to use the new technology this way and to modernize the law and the business models involved. We should change our way of looking at books on legal grounds. Indeed if we continue to see the book as an object of property and if we stay collectively stuck in the field of property law, we will naturally be tempted to repeat in the virtual book market our attitude toward tangible goods that exist in a limited amount. Such an approach to the virtual book is not favorable to its flow in the global market. In the virtual economy, there are no limits to the creation of intellectual wealth, and the concept of property is not suited to this context of information affluence. The best course would be to forget about intellectual property, incorporeal property or literary property as fictitious legal concepts that were politically correct a long time ago but are now misleading generations of lawyers and the public authorities they counsel.

If we keep speaking in terms of intellectual property, the chances are high that the new technologies will be used contrary to their purpose in order to create an artificial information scarcity. If such a creation continues, we will all forfeit the benefit of technological progress. Worse, the market is at high risk should all technological controls, now centralized, be cracked. Instead, if e-books are slightly protected but extremely cheap, readers will not be interested in piracy and hackers will be much less interested in cracking these codes. Prior to being an object, a book is a message, that is to say ideas circulating among people. This approach to the book naturally involves the category of personal rights more suited to the virtual world. The Internet in general should be approached with a strategy focused on human relationships, with the generous aim of favoring cultural abundance for all. DRM technologies, like all other technologies, are not 100 % reliable and will never be. They will never replace a good copyright law, innovative, focused on people and above all welcome by the readership.

2: Copyright law must be focused on persons and not objects

We should become more aware of the role played by the readership in the process of the protection of authors' rights. Persons and their balanced relationships should be at the heart of a modernized copyright law. What matters is not in fact protecting objects of property, but balancing relationships. Even if information technology and criminal law can help, the main point of an efficient copyright strategy should be focused on balancing people's relationships with regard to intellectual works. A modern copyright law should deter people from acting parasitically to authors. Law should use prevention means and punishments too. A modernized copyright law, combined with the business strategy of low priced e-books, will render piracy of books and e-books less interesting. This fact is important if we wish to preserve the future of the book market and increase its prosperity.

Current copyright laws have become too complex because they focus on objects (books), storage mediums and reproduction tools that are constantly changing due to new technologies. Such complexity plays an important role in the legal inefficiency. It would be much better to replace all this complexity with a more simple copyright law based on the balance of people's relationships. This approach would make the domestic and international modernization of copyright laws much easier. Copyright law of the French Revolution[59] focused on people and we can still gain from the wisdom it contains that we have lost in our world of technological sophistication. This copyright law was simple, went directly to the essential points, and was pragmatically efficient. This law was focused on people and dealt with actions permitted and actions prohibited. Prohibited actions were what we today call piracy or parasitism. Initiated in Switzerland,[60] French

98

and Belgian courts use "la théorie des agissements parasitaires" (theory of piracy practices) when they want to protect the investments and work of a creator from parasitism of others. In such cases, they check whether there is a prejudice to the detriment of the creator, if there is a link between the action of a person and the prejudice, and also if the infringing person has gained from this parasitism. This legal doctrine, combined to the Anglo-American concept of fair use,[61] is the path to follow in order to set up a simpler and more efficient domestic and international copyright law. Instead of being focused on the supposed objects of an impossible intellectual property, this modernized copyright law would reinitiate the dialogue between readers and the book industry, and make them aware of their own role and responsibility in creating cultural affluence. In this way, we would escape the current bad situation in the book market, when readers are simultaneously potential customers who should be tempted to buy and potential enemies who should be rigorously controlled and severely punished.

3: **The concept of parasitism (piracy practices) must prevail over the definition of protected objects**

Piracy in itself, accomplished with whichever present or future tool or means, should be legally punished (and deterred) as soon as parasitic actions become harmful to authors and to the collectivity. When authors suffer piracy from readers, this ends up in decreasing information wealth for all. In order to be able to punish parasitic actions, the law must organize the means of proof.

4: **Public authorities worldwide should organize the ways to prove the existence, the original content and the authorship of books**

Nowadays, one of the advantages of the legal deposit in some countries and of copyright in others, is the provision of proof of the existence of books and of their authorship. Countries could continue with their own practices, but technology should help improve them by allowing digital deposit of works. A worldwide digital catalogue that is not centralized but networked should also be set up. Registration of works in this international database should be free and open to all and a board should be charged to control its fair use. The existing technology already makes this kind of initiative possible. This catalogue should not be centralized but networked among all the countries of the world. An international networked legal deposit of digital works would also be of interest and would achieve the old dream of a universal library. Such a legal deposit would contribute to increasing and organizing human knowledge as a whole, and would facilitate access to knowledge to even the poorest or geographically most isolated communities in the world. Instead of investing in sophisticated devices to control readers, the book industry should better invest in efficient and intuitive search tools, and in making e-books more attractive. States on their side should focus on justice.

5: States must favor justice

States should use their powers to favor justice in the virtual book market. We mean justice as we have defined it for the virtual world. Justice as the art of sharing, scarcity is useless in the virtual world. Instead, justice in the virtual world is the art of accelerating the information flow that in turn creates prosperity. Thus, the role of States should be to take all preventive and punitive

101

measures to favor the free flow of ideas. States must therefore intervene to fight any attempt to hinder the circulation of e-books.[62] One of the most important obstacles comes from the State's will to levy tax on the emerging virtual book market. States worldwide are more focused on making money through taxing virtual exchanges, than on favoring the use of the new technologies to create prosperity.[63] States are wrong when they use significant public budgets on technology to control Internet flows and their citizens. They are not sure of being paid back and not even sure that this technology will be efficient enough. On the other hand, if this technology of control actually became efficient, it would put States' power at risk![64] Indeed, if they become commonplace, electronic means of control set up by the States would be tempting for terrorists wishing to take control (and money from) people instead of them. States would make a better choice if they favored the expansion of the virtual book market by making it free of tax. This would help the e-book market succeed and boost creation of material wealth in many other fields. It would be much better for States to levy tax on a wealthier material world than on an (impoverished) virtual economy. Tax strategies should be revised.

6: States must revise their tax strategy

States should take any possible initiative to favor the use of new technologies for accelerating the flow of ideas. It is clear that if they levy tax on this market, this would considerably slow down the circulation of e-books and bring to the market a complexity that could be avoided. Tax levying requires control over citizens; it involves centralization and may also favor intrusion into citizens' privacy. (Through all these controls, for example, States can control what people read). State taxes on e-books make them more expensive (in France they amount to 19.6% of the list price, when tax is only 5.5% on printed books) and if States, wholesalers, distributors, booksellers, banks, etc., want to levy money on e-books, it would be impossible to sell them at very low prices and the chances are extremely high that we will all forfeit the benefit of technological progress.[65]

CONCLUSION

The way we perceive books, authors, the publishing market, is strongly marked by History. Technology has evolved much more rapidly than mentalities. Copyright laws throughout the world were created for printed books sold within domestic territories, and are not suited to a virtual world where intangible books are sold worldwide through the Internet. In the virtual book market, some key concepts of copyright law have become obsolete, among them, the traditional idea of justice and the concept of intellectual property. In order that all the links of the book chain, from the author to the reader, become open to the much better possibilities offered by communication technologies, we should change our attitude toward the virtual world. We should adapt our business, economic, governmental and social strategies to the specific functioning of the virtual world, instead of trying to impose on it our old habits from the material world. We already own the technology that can allow us to say goodbye to a publishing world marked by the logic of scarcity, the exclusion of too many authors and their ideas, the frustration of too many people, the poverty of too many public libraries. We now have the technological tools to create a world of actual freedom of speech and of information affluence, as part of a wealthier book market.

NOTES

[1] *Le droit d'auteur et l'Internet*, Rapport du groupe de travail de l'Académie des Sciences Morales et Politiques présidé par M. Gabriel DE BROGLIE, p. 6: Translation from French: "L'objet de ce rapport est d'analyser les incidences sur le droit d'auteur de ce nouveau moyen de communication (Internet) et de dresser un état des lieux du respect du droit d'auteur et des droits voisins dans les nouvelles technologies de l'information."

[2] *Ibid.*, p. 8. Translation from French: "Il semble en réalité que les solides principes du droit d'auteur et des droits voisins appellent, dans l'environnement numérique, une simple adaptation plus qu'un bouleversement."

[3] *Ibid.*, p. 27. Translation from French: "La législation sur le droit d'auteur s'applique donc à l'Internet."

[4] *Ibid.*, p. 36. Translation from French: "En définitive, l'application de la législation relative au droit d'auteur n'est pas impossible, mais se heurte dans la pratique, à de nombreuses difficultés. Les composantes traditionnelles du droit d'auteur sont bouleversées, ses limitations légales tendent à devenir tout autre chose que des exceptions, et même la détermination du droit applicable ne va pas

sans difficulté. Mais, sur toutes les questions précédemment abordées, la législation existe."

[5] 360 BC, PHAEDRUS, by Plato, translated by Benjamin Jowett
http://philosophy.eserver.org/plato/phaedrus.txt

[6] MANCINI Anna, *Maat Revealed, Philosophy of Justice in Ancient Egypt*, USA, Buenos Books America, 2005.

[7] MANCINI Anna, *Ancient Roman Solutions to Modern Legal Issues, The example of Patent Law*, USA, Buenos Books America, 2004.

[8] 360 BC, PHAEDRUS, by Plato, translated by Benjamin Jowett
http://philosophy.eserver.org/plato/phaedrus.txt

[9] FISCHER Steven Roger, *A History of Reading*, London UK, Reaktion Books, 2003, p. 89, p. 351 Augustine of Hippo, 'Of the Origin and Nature of the Soul', in Basic Writings of Saint Augustine, ed. Whitney J; Oates (London, 1948), IV:7:9"
See also Alberto Manguel, Chapter 2 of *A History of Reading*(New York; Viking, 1996)
http://www.stanford.edu/class/history34q/readings/Manguel/Silent_Readers.html

[10] FISCHER, Steven Roger, *op. cit.,* p. 95.

[11] KANT Immanual, The science of right, translated by W. HASTIE, http://www.eserver.org

[12] FISCHER Steven Roger, *op. cit.,* 2003, p. 176.

[13] FISCHER Steven Roger, *op. cit.,* 2003, p. 195.

[14] MANCINI Anna, *Internet Justice, Philosophy of Law for the Virtual World,* USA, Buenos Books America, 2005.

[15] MANCINI Anna, *Internet Justice, op. cit.,* 2005.

[16] On the history of the concept of universal library and on its application to the concept of virtual library,

cf. James J. O'DONNELL, *Avatars Of The Word, From Papyrus To Cyberspace*, Cambridge, Mass., Harvard University Press, 1998. See also information on the modern project of worldwide library by Google: Google Books
http://print.google.com/support/publisher/bin/index.py ?fulldump=1

[17] BARRÉ Martine, "L'OMPI et la Mondialisation du droit de la Propriété Intellectuelle", in *La mondialisation du droit*, Sous la direction d'Eric LOQUIN et Catherine KESSEDJIAN, Travaux du Centre de Recherche sur le droit des marchés et des investissements internationaux, Book 19, LITEC, 2000, p. 277-295.

[18] And also to abundance and not to scarcity. Contrary to the incorrect analysis of many, copyright law does not contribute to the creation of scarcity.

[19] And also STEFIK Mark, *The Internet Edge, Social, Legal and Technological Challenges for a Networked World*, MIT, 1999, p. 106: "Without trusted systems, digital publishing is at risk."

[20] According to the report issued by the French Council of State (Conseil d'Etat) the majority of professionals believe that the devices used to secure works will allow piracy to be dealt with efficiently. Conseil d'Etat, France, *op. cit.,* 2 July 1998, p. 117.

[21] *Internet Justice, op. cit.*

[22] Conseil d'Etat, *op. cit.:*Translated from French: "Il n'y a d'économie que lorsqu'il y a rareté et attrait pour cette rareté de la part du public." " Dans le cas du livre imprimé, chaque objet a son prix. Le livre objet, c'est un univers de rareté, dont l'équation économique est claire. La création de contenus est rémunérée. Le support physique permet cette

rémunération.... La numérisation de la monnaie permet le paiement dans un univers numérique. Il convient donc de mettre en oeuvre des solutions techniques, créatrices de rareté."

[23] Gordon GRAHAM, *As I was saying, Essays on the international book business*, UK, Hans Zell Publishers, 1994, p. 190: "The book is not fundamentally in danger. It will continue to flourish, and should be improved by the electronic devices not only in terms of production, but also of distribution. A totally new electronic publishing industry will grow side by side with folio publishing and create new markets."

[24] J. O'DONNELL James, *op.cit.*, p. 90.

[25] LUCAS André, *Droit d'auteur et numérique*, Paris, Litec, 1998, p. 100, quoted in DE BROGLIE report, p. 38.

[26] KELSEN Hans, *Introduction to the problems of legal theory, A translation of the First Edition of the Reine Rechtslehre or Pure Theory of Law*, translated by Bonnie LITSCHEVESKI PAULSON and Stanley L. PAULSON, Oxford, Clarendon Press, 1992.

[27] MANCINI Anna, *Internet Justice, op. cit.*

[28] On this last point see: *Où vont les autoroutes de l'information*, under the direction Marc GUILLAUME, Commissariat Général du Plan, Commission Européenne, Paris, Descartes & Cie, 1997, p. 117-118.

[29] See on this point: Francis LORENTZ, *La nouvelle donne du commerce électronique: réalisations 1998 et perspectives: rapport de la mission Commerce électronique*, France, Ministère de l'économie, des finances et de l'industrie, Paris, Éditions de Bercy, Études ISSN 1245-2246, 1999, I.2.7.

http://www.telecom.gouv.fr/francais/activ/techno/tech
ndoc/technodoc.htm

[30] Bill GATES, *Business @ the speed of Thought*,
London, Penguin Books, 1999, p. 2.

[31] See: Michael LEGAT, *An author's guide to
publishing*, London, Robert Hale, 3rd edition, 1998,
p. 41-42.

[32] Andrew B. WHINSTON, Dale O. STAHL, Soon-
Yong CHOI, *The Economics of Electronic
Commerce,* Macmillan Technical Publishing,
Indianapolis, Indiana, 1997, p. 176.

[33] Geoffrey BROWN, *The Information Game, Ethical
Issues in a Microchip, World*, NJ and London,
Humanities Press International, 1990, p. 115.

[34] ROSE Mark, "The author as proprietor: Donaldson
V. Becket and the Genealogy of Modern Authorship",
Of Authors and Origins, Essays on Copyright Law,
Brad SHERMAN and Alain STROWEL, Oxford,
Clarendon Press, 1994, p. 23-55.

[35] Andrew B. WHINSTON, Dale O. STAHL, Soon-
Yong CHOI, *The Economics of Electronic
Commerce*, Indiana, Indianapolis, Macmillan
Technical Publishing, *op. cit.*, p. 179.

[36] *Internet Law and Regulation*, Edited by Graham
JH Smith, Bird & Bird, London, Second edition,
Published by FT Law & Tax, 1997, p. 13. "Intellectual
property laws govern the substance and scope of
property rights in the intangible fruits of human
creativity and labor: writing, drama, music and art....
Appropriately defined property rights help to
transform those fruits into money, another intangible.
Digitalization enables both the raw fruits and their
monetary products to be reduced to bits of
information stored electronically and routed around

111

networks." *Cf.* also: Christopher MILLARD, *Computer law*, Third Edition, Edited by Chris Reed, Blackstone Press limited,1996, "...information is normally very valuable, and in general most things which have a market value are dealt with by the law as a species of property." *Cf.* the French code of Intellectual Property (Code de la propriété intellectuelle), states (article L; 111-1 of the first chapter dedicated to the nature of the author's right): "The author of a work of the mind has on this work, as soon as it is created, a right of incorporeal property exclusive and opposable to all." (translated from French: "L'auteur d'une oeuvre de l'esprit jouit sur cette oeuvre, du seul fait de sa création, d'un droit de propriété incorporelle exclusif et opposable à tous."). The code also states (article L. 111-3):"The incorporeal property defined in the article L. 111-1 is independent from the property of the physical object." (translated from French: "La propriété incorporelle définie par l'article L. 111-1 est indépendante de la propriété de l'objet matériel".)

[37] On the history of copyright law from Antiquity until the present day, see: Marie-Claude DOCK, "Genèse et évolution de la notion de propriété littéraire", p. 127-206, Brad SHERMAN and Alain STROWEL, *Of Authors and Origins, Essays on Copyright Law*, Oxford, Clarendon Press, 1994; *Histoire internationale du droit d'auteur des origines à nos jours*, Paris, Revue Internationale du Droit d'Auteur, janvier 1974; Eugène POUILLET, *Traité théorique et pratique de la propriété littéraire et artistique et du droit de représentation*, 3ème édition, Paris, Marchal et Billard, 1908, p. 1-22; Henri FALK, *Les privilèges de librairie sous l'ancien régime*, Paris, Thèse, 1906;

Didier PHILIPPON, *Des anciens privilèges de librairie*, Paris, 1955.

[38] Detailed studies of these doctrines in: Pierre RECHT, *Le droit d'auteur, une nouvelle forme de propriété*, Paris, LGDJ, 1969.

[39] Pierre RECHT, *Le droit d'auteur, une nouvelle forme de propriété*, Paris, LGDJ, 1969, p. 93. See also: Paul Edward GELLER, "Conflicts of law in cyberspace: International copyright in a digitally networked world", in *The future of copyright in a digital environment*, editor P. Bernt HUGENHOLTZ, Proceedings of the Royal Academy Colloquium, Amsterdam, 6-7 July 1995, The Hague, London, Boston, KLUWER LAW INTERNATIONAL, 1996, p. 27-48, p. 42.

[40] Eugène POUILLET, *Traité théorique et pratique de la propriété littéraire et artistique et du droit de représentation*, 3rd edition, Paris, Marchal et Billard, 1908, p. 26.

[41] History of copyright law in England is also significant. *Cf.* Mark ROSE, « The author as proprietor: Donaldson v. Becket and the Genealogy of Modern Authorship", p. 23-55, in *Of Authors and Origins, Essays on Copyright Law*, Brad SHERMAN and Alain STROWEL, Clarendon Press, Oxford. *Cf.* André Françon, *La propriété littéraire et artistique en Grande-Bretagne et aux Etats-Unis*, Paris, 1955, Marie-Claude DOCK, "Genèse et évolution de la notion de propriété littéraire", *Histoire internationale du droit d'auteur des origines à nos jours*, Paris, Revue Internationale du Droit d'Auteur, January 1974, p. 127-206.

[42] In the same line *cf.* Marie CORNU, "Droit de la culture et mondialisation de l'économie", *La*

113

mondialisation du droit, under the direction of Eric LOQUIN and Catherine KESSEDJIAN, Travaux du Centre de Recherche sur le droit des marchés et des investissements internationaux, Book 19, LITEC, 2000, p. 551-596, p. 576.

[43] Quoted in Mark ROSE, p 29, *cf.* Richard D. ALTICK, *The English Common Reader* (Chicago, 1957), notamment. P. 30-36, on the development of the book market.

[44] In 1710, in England, in the Statute of Anne, *cf.* Roger CHARTIER, "Figures of the Author", p. 7-22, in: *Of Authors and Origins, Essays on Copyright Law,* Brad SHERMAN and Alain STROWEL, Clarendon Press, Oxford, 1994, p. 13; André FRANçON, *La Propriété littéraire et artistique en Grande-Bretagne et aux Etats-Unis,* Paris, 1955, p. 9; from 1761, in France, *cf.* Claude COLOMBET, *op. cit.,* p. 4.

[45] Booksellers were also publishers, they constituted at this time the entire book chain. *Cf.* on this point: Marie-Claude DOCK, "Genèse et évolution de la notion de propriété littéraire", p. 127-206, in *Histoire internationale du droit d'auteur des origines à nos jours,* Paris, Revue Internationale du Droit d'Auteur, janvier 1974, p. 159, note 50; *cf.* Pierre-Yves GAUTIER, *Propriété littéraire et artistique,* Paris, PUF, 3rd edition,1991, p. 18.

[46] Loi et Actes du Gouvernement, 1st Book, Paris, Imprimerie Royale, 1834, p. 1-5.

[47] On privileges before the French Revolution *cf.* Pierre-Yves GAUTIER, *Propriété littéraire et artistique,* Paris, PUF, 3rd edition,1991, p. 19.

[48] *Cf.* for the use of the concept of property in the USA: Valerio DE SANCTIS, "Le développement et la

consécration internationale du droit d'auteur", *Histoire internationale du droit d'auteur des origines à nos jours*, Paris, Revue Internationale du Droit d'Auteur, January 1974, p. 207-291, p. 209. Copyright law enacted during the Revolution can be found in: Eugène POUILLET, *op. cit.*, 879 and 880 for the decrees of 13 and 19 January 1791, (the law published in this source is the one slightly amended by the law of 11 March 1902). The text of the law of 19 January 1793 can be found in*: Lois et actes du gouvernement,* Paris, Imprimerie Royale, 1834, book VII, p. 203.

[49] On the link between the emergence of the concept of property and the will to maintain privileges, see: Roger CHARTIER, "Figures of the Author", *Of Authors and Origins, Essays on Copyright Law*, Brad SHERMAN and Alain STROWEL, Clarendon Press, Oxford, 1994, p. 7-22, p. 12.

[50] *Cf.* French Code of Intellectual Property (Code de la propriété intellectuelle), states (article L; 111-1 of the first chapter dedicated to the nature of the author's right): "The author of a work of the mind has on this work, as soon as it is created, a right of incorporeal property exclusive and opposable to all." (translated from French: "L'auteur d'une oeuvre de l'esprit jouit sur cette oeuvre, du seul fait de sa création, d'un droit de propriété incorporelle exclusif et opposable à tous."). The code also states (article L. 111-3):"The incorporeal property defined in the article L. 111-1 is independent from the property of the physical object." (translated from French: "La propriété incorporelle définie par l'article L. 111-1 est indépendante de la propriété de l'objet matériel".)

[51] Pierre BOURDIEU, Ce que parler veut dire, l'économie des échanges linguistiques, Paris, Fayard, 1982, p. 20 Translated from French: "...le droit le plus rigoureusement rationalisé n'est jamais qu'un acte de magie sociale qui réussit."

[52] Pierre-Yves GAUTIER, *op. cit.*, p. 22, Claude COLOMBET, *op. cit.*, p. 10.

[53] About the privileges, *cf.* Pierre-Yves GAUTIER, *Propriété littéraire et artistique*, Paris, PUF, 3ème édition,1991.

[54] Mark ROSE,"The author as proprietor: Donaldson v. Becket and the Genealogy of Modern Authorship", *Of Authors and Origins, Essays on Copyright Law*, Brad SHERMAN and Alain STROWEL, Clarendon Press, Oxford, 1994, p. 23-55, p. 39.

[55] Emmanuel KANT, *op. cit.*, p. 169, p. 170. See also: Marie CORNU, "Droit de la culture et mondialisation de l'économie", *La mondialisation du droit, op. cit.*, p. 551-596, p. 576: She notices the strong personal aspect of culture and its laws.

[56] *Cf.* Marie CORNU, "Droit de la culture et mondialisation de l'économie", *op. cit.:* p. 551-596, p. 569.

[57] Mark STEFIK, *The Internet Edge, Social, Legal and Technological Challenges for a Networked World*, Cambridge, Mass, MIT press, 1999, p. 80.

[58] LESSIG Lawrence, *Code and Other Laws of Cyberspace*, Basic Books, 2000.

[59] *Cf.* law of 19 July 1793, in: *Lois et actes du gouvernement*, Paris, Imprimerie Royale, 1834, book VII, p. 203.

[60] Current case law trend in France and Belgium is toward a wider admission of this theory, in France, on the basis of article 1382 of the Civil Code. This

trend is spreading to many intellectual creations protected or unprotected by existing systems of legal privileges (i.e., authors' rights, patent law).
See. mainly SAINT-GALL (Yves), "Concurrence déloyale et concurrence parasitaire (ou agissements parasitaires)", Revue Internationale de la Propriété Industrielle et Artistique, n° 25-26, 1956; LE TOURNEAU (Philippe), Traité de la Responsabilité civile, éd. Dalloz 1982; DESJEUX (Xavier) "Le droit de la responsabilité civile comme limite au principe de la liberté du commerce et de l'industrie (à propos de la sanction de la copie)", SJ CDE, n° 22, 30 May 1985, II 14490. See also, "The liability in French and Belgian laws of search tools in the Internet", International Journal of Law and Information Technology 1999 7(3):238-255; doi:10.1093/ijlit/7.3.238

[61] On parasitism of intellectual works in French case law see: "Le parasitisme dans la jurisprudence (française) au titre de l'usurpation des 'investissements intellectuels' d'un tiers, Michel VIVANT, *Les créations immatérielles et le droit*, Paris, Ellipses, 1997, pp. 20-21. For a comparison with the application of the anglo-american concept of fair use, *cf.* Paul Edward GELLER, "Conflicts of law in cyberspace: International copyright in a digitally networked world", *op. cit.,* p. 43.

[62] This should be also true for any kind of books.

[63] The report issued by the French Council of State (Conseil d'Etat français) underlines the importantce for the French State to levy VAT which amounts to 18,6 % of State income» (In French: "Les enjeux sont considérables pour les Etats membres de l'Union européenne sur lesquels pèse un réel risque

budgétaire -la TVA représente en effet 18,6% de leurs recettes fiscales-, même si les risques ne sont pas immédiats, compte tenu notamment du volume modéré actuellement du commerce électronique.", Conseil d'Etat, France, *op. cit., 2 juillet 1998*, Paris, La Documentation française, 1998, p. 73.

[64] *Cf.* on the difficulty to set up automatic VAT levy on the Internet: Conseil d'Etat, France, *Internet et les réseaux numériques, étude adoptée par l'Assemblée générale du Conseil d'Etat le 2 juillet 1998*, Paris, La Documentation française, 1998, p. 74.

[65] When an e-book is very cheap there is no longer interest for the public to pirate it, to borrow it from a friend, to copy of photocopy it, or to read it for free in a public library.

BIBLIOGRAPHY

BROWN Geoffrey, *The Information Game, Ethical Issues in a Microchip, World*, NJ and London, Humanities Press International, 1990

CHARTIER Roger, "Figures of the Author", in *Of Authors and Origins, Essays on Copyright Law*, Brad SHERMAN and Alain STROWEL, Clarendon Press, Oxford, 1994, p. 7-22,

FISCHER, Steven Roger, *A History of Reading*, London UK, Reaktion Books, 2003

GOLSTEIN Paul, *Copyright's Highway: From Gutenberg to the Celestial Jukebox,* Stanford Law School; 2003

GRAHAM Gordon, *As I was saying, Essays on the international book business*, UK, Hans Zell Publishers, 1994

GUIBAULT Lucie M.C.R., *Copyright Limitations and Contracts: An Analysis of the Contractual Overridability of Limitations on Copyright*, Kluwer Law International, 2002

HUGENHOLTZ P. Bernt editor, *The future of copyright in a digital environment*, Proceedings of the Royal

Academy Colloquium, Amsterdam, 6-7 July 1995, The Hague, London, Boston, KLUWER LAW INTERNATIONAL, 1996.

KOEPSELL David R., *The Ontology of Cyberspace: Philosophy, Law, and the Future of Intellectual Property*,, Open Court Publishing Company, 2003

LESSIG Lawrence, *Code and Other Laws of Cyberspace*, Basic Books, 2000

LESSIG Lawrence, *Free Culture, How Big Media Uses Technology and the Law to Lock Down Culture and Control Creativity*, Penguin Press HC, 2004

LITMAN Jessica, *Digital Copyright: Protecting Intellectual Property on the Internet*, Prometheus Books, 2000

O'DONNELL James J., *Avatars of the word, From Papyrus to Cyberspace*, Cambridge, Mass., Harvard University Press, 1998.

ROSE Mark, "The author as proprietor: Donaldson v. Becket and the Genealogy of Modern Authorship", *Of Authors and Origins, Essays on Copyright Law*, Brad SHERMAN and Alain STROWEL, Oxford, Clarendon Press, 1994, p. 23-55

ROSE Mark, *Authors and Owners : The Invention of Copyright*, Harvard University Press; 1995

120

SANCHIS MARTINEZ Maria Trinidad, *Derechos de Autor, Digitalizacion e Internet*, Editorial Universitas SA, Madrid, 2004

SHERMAN Brad and STROWEL Alain, *Of Authors and Origins, Essays on Copyright Law*, Oxford, Clarendon Press, 1994

STEFIK Mark, *The Internet Edge, Social, Legal and Technological Challenges for a Networked World*, MIT, 1999

VAIDHYANATHAN Siva, *Copyrights and Copywrongs: The Rise of Intellectual Property and How It Threatens Creativity*, New York University Press, 2003

VAIDHYANATHAN Siva, *The Anarchist in the Library: How the Clash Between Freedom and Control is Hacking the Real World and Crashing the System*, Basic Books, 2004

By the same Author:

MAAT REVEALED, PHILOSOPHY OF JUSTICE IN ANCIENT EGYPT

ISBN: 1-932848-10-X (PAPERBACK) ENGLISH
132 pages, 25 USD
ISBN: 1-932848-11-8 (E-BOOK) ENGLISH

Categories: Egyptology, philosophy of law, history of religions

Unlike ancient Rome, Egypt did not transmit any legal system to us, but rather an idea of justice our modern minds can hardly understand. In the ancient Egyptian world, almost all the texts and inscriptions speak of justice. All the texts of wisdom teach that one has to conform to Maat, an obscure and omnipresent concept that Egyptologists have translated into the expression "Goddess of Truth and Justice".

Egyptian justice is so different from ours that Egyptologists and historians of religions believe they have not yet fully understood its meaning. They regret this fact because understanding Maat would be a gateway to a deeper understanding of the ancient Egyptian world. As for lawyers, they have limited themselves to the Greco-Roman sources on the philosophy of Justice and the discoveries of Egyptologists in this philosophical field remain thoroughly ignored. Thanks to her experience in ancient history of law and her ability to understand ancient symbols, the author provides Egyptology with the missing pieces that were needed to form a coherent image of Maat. Once revealed, Maat sheds a new and unexpected light on the whole of Egyptian civilization. As a bridge between traditionally separate fields of academic research, this book is a useful and groundbreaking contribution to Egyptology, the history of religions and the modern philosophy of law.

Anna MANCINI, Ph. D
Buenos Books America
WWW. BUENOSBOOKSAMERICA.COM

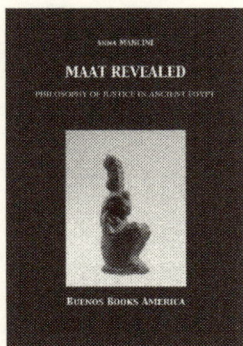